MALE SPORTS STARS

CHELSEA HOUSE PUBLISHERS

MALE SPORTS STARS

SUPERSTARS OF MEN'S TRACK AND FIELD

Fred McMane

CHELSEA HOUSE PUBLISHERS
Philadelphia

Produced by Daniel Bial and Associates
New York, New York

Picture research by Alan Gottlieb
Cover illustration by Bradford Brown
frontispiece photo: Carl Lewis

First Printing

1 3 5 7 9 8 6 4 2

Library of Congress Cataloging-in-Publication Data

McMane, Fred.
        Superstars of men's track & field / Fred McMane.
            p.   cm. — (Male sports stars)
        Includes bibliographical references (p.) and index.
        Summary: A brief overview of track and field competitions precedes
profiles of six champions: Bob Mathias, Roger Bannister, Al Oerter,
Edwin Moses, Carl Lewis, and Michael Johnson.
            ISBN 0-7910-4591-9 (hc)
            1. Track and field athletes—Biography—Juvenile literature.
[1. Track and field athletes.] I. Title. II. Series.
GV697.A1M2616   1998
796.42'081'092—dc21
[B]   97-42869
                                                                        CIP
                                                                         AC

CONTENTS

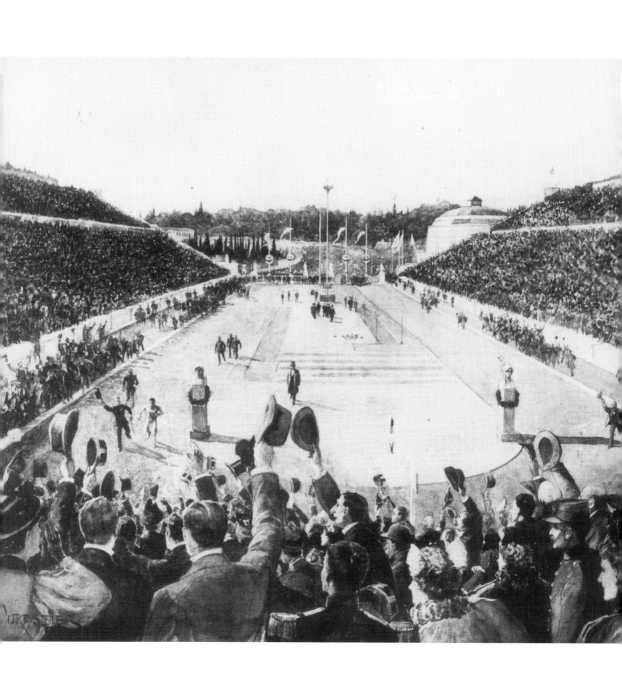

Track and field is sport in its purest form. The first one across the finish line wins; the one who throws the farthest or jumps the best is champion.

While competitions have been held throughout the centuries, the most famous are the Olympic Games. They may have begun around 1370 B.C. as small events held on a grassy plain near the Temple of Zeus in Olympia, and they may have been an outgrowth of a religious rite. The first documented Olympic Games—or rather Game—occurred in 776 B.C., and there was only one event, a footrace the length of the stadium, which was about 186 yards. Other events were soon added, such as the discus, javelin, and long jump.

The last ancient Olympics was held in 393 A.D.

In 1896, the first modern Olympic Games were held in Athens, Greece. This drawing, based on a famous photo, shows the crowd cheering for the winner of the marathon (lower left).

Emperor Theodosius of Rome abolished them after that for religious and political reasons. In the centuries following, track and field events were mostly held at military tournaments. It wasn't until the 1800s that track and field competition as we know it today evolved. In 1837 in England, Eton College held a track meet between two classes. Many races in the early days of track and field were started by "mutual consent." This meant that the runners took off when all were ready. Sometimes, starts were delayed for a long time because one runner would try to outfox the other to get a better start. In fact, an early rule required the use of a starter's pistol only if the start by mutual consent didn't occur within an hour.

In 1892, a wealthy Frenchman named Baron Pierre de Coubertin proposed the idea of starting a modern Olympic Games in order to promote international goodwill through athletic competition. He spent the next three and a half years drumming up support. Since interest was the greatest in Greece it was decided that the first modern Olympic Games would be held in Athens in 1896.

Georgios Averoff, a wealthy architect, put up one million drachma ($184,000) to build a new stadium, and additional money was raised by the sale of souvenir stamps and medals. In addition to track and field, competition was held in swimming, tennis, weight lifting, shooting, fencing, and cycling.

The Games from 1900 to 1908 produced the first international track and field hero. His name was Ray Ewry, a hydraulics engineer who worked for the New York City Water Department. Ewry's specialty was the standing jump, and he scored a perfect 10 in his specialty, winning 10 gold medals in 10 events.

Ewry won gold medals in the standing long jump, standing high jump, and standing triple jump in 1900 and 1904. The standing triple jump was eliminated after 1904, but Ewry won both the standing long jump and standing high jump at the 1906 Intercalated Games and the 1908 Olympic Games in London. After 1912, the standing jumps were removed from competition in favor of jumps from a running start. So Ewry is in the record books as the only athlete ever to have won the standing jump events—a perfect 10 for 10.

With athletes like Ewry, who captained the Purdue University track and field team, the sport began to grow in popularity during the early part of the 20th century, especially on the collegiate level. In 1908, a young football player at an Indian trade school in Carlisle, Pennsylvania, was persuaded by his football coach to go out for the track team and in a very short time would bring international recognition to the sport. His name was Jim Thorpe.

Jim Thorpe was born in Shawnee, Oklahoma, and was a member of the Sac and Fox Indian tribe. His father was half-Indian and half-Irish; his mother was the granddaughter of Black Hawk, the famous Chippewa chief, and was also part French. During his teenage years, he was sent to the Indian training school in Kansas. But he was unhappy there. When his father died, he ran away from school and found his way back to Shawnee. Government officials in the territory then decided to send him to Carlisle Institute, an Indian trade school in Pennsylvania. The school was much farther away and it would be harder to return. In 1904, Jim left for Carlisle to take courses in tailoring. But he was destined for other things.

Although only 4'10" and 115 pounds when he arrived at Carlisle at age 15, he grew bigger and stronger in his first couple of years there and became a star football player by 1908. One spring day in 1908, Jim was observing a track and field practice and noticed that the high-jumpers were having trouble getting over the bar. Pop Warner, the Carlisle football and track coach, asked Jim to try the jump. Jim was wearing overalls and sneakers, but he easily cleared the bar.

Warner told Jim that if he could clear 5'9" in the high jump he could join the team for the next meet. Jim easily cleared the height and promptly joined the track team. He found that he excelled at other events, too, and easily beat the best sprinters and hurdlers on the team. He was even the best at the javelin throw, even though he had never thrown one before.

In his first track meet against a powerful team from Lafayette University, Jim won seven events. Later in the season, against an even stronger team from Harvard, Jim won all eight events he entered.

In 1912, Jim represented the United States in the Olympic Games and turned in one of the most remarkable performances in history. He won gold medals in both the decathlon and pentathlon. He won seven of the 10 events in the decathlon and four of the five events in the pentathlon. He returned to the United States a hero.

His good fortune was short-lived, however. A few months after the close of the his last football season, a Massachusetts newspaper reported that Jim had played professional baseball in

Jim Thorpe, shown here wearing his Olympic uniform, won two gold medals at the 1912 Olympics in Stockholm.

1909 for a minor league team and so could not be considered an amateur. Jim admitted he had played for two seasons for a minor league team in North Carolina. He was unaware that such a thing was illegal.

Thorpe went on to play professional football and major league baseball, but he was forced to give back the medals he had won in the Olympics. It took his family many years of campaigning to get his records reinstated and his medals returned. Unfortunately, Jim did not live to see it. He died on March 28, 1953, two months shy of his 65th birthday. The International Olympic Committee did not approve Thorpe's reinstatement until 1982.

In 1912, 16 countries agreed to form the International Amateur Athletic Federation (IAAF) in order to better control the rules and regulations

*Paavo Nurmi, "the Flying
Finn," was one of the greatest
long-distance runners. He
won nine gold medals at
three different Olympics.*

of the sport. It is still the governing body of the
sport today.

Until Carl Lewis came along in the 1980s,
Jesse Owens was probably the most recognized
athlete in track and field. The son of Alabama
sharecroppers, Jesse moved with his family to
Cleveland when he was nine years old, and by
the time he reached high school, he was a national star in track and field. He set national records
in the 100- and 220-yard dashes and in the long
jump.

In 1935, while competing for Ohio State in the Big Ten championships at Ann Arbor, Michigan, Owens had one of the greatest meets ever. He broke five world records and equaled a sixth in the space of 45 minutes. But that was nothing compared to the heights he would reach at the 1936 Olympic Games in Berlin, Germany.

Adolf Hitler had become chancellor of Germany, and his Nazi party preached that blacks and Jews were inferior to whites, especially those of the Germanic, or Aryan, race. Owens, a black man, exploded those myths by winning four gold medals in the Games. He won the 100-meter, 200-meter, and long-jump titles and anchored the winning 4 x 100-meter relay team.

Owens returned home from his Olympic triumphs to a hero's welcome and a ticker tape parade down Broadway. However, he was snubbed by President Roosevelt, who never even sent a letter of congratulations, and by the Amateur Athletic Union (AAU), which bypassed him for the Sullivan Award, given to the nation's best amateur athlete, in favor of decathlon champion Glenn Morris.

Owens's Olympic gold medals did not bring him instant fortune either. He struggled for nearly two decades trying to make ends meet before finally achieving financial security as a public speaker on behalf of various corporate sponsors. He died of lung cancer in 1980 at the age of 66.

Today, meets are sponsored by large companies that award prize money. Because they can now earn a living in their sport, track and field athletes can compete longer than in the past. One wonders what athletes like Jim Thorpe and Jesse Owens might have achieved under similar rules.

2

BOB MATHIAS: KING OF THE DECATHLON

Born in Tulare, California, on November 19, 1930, Bob Mathias showed standout athletic ability in the early stages of his life, displaying "an amazing sense of coordination" almost from infancy. Before he was six years old, he had earned a place in his older brother's baseball games.

At Tulare High School, Bob became a star fullback on the football team, the leading scorer on the basketball team, and the best track and field performer in the state. He was also president of his senior class. During his high school track and field career, he won 40 events and broke 21 records.

When he was 16, Bob entered the West Coast Relays in Fresno. He won the shot put, the discus throw, and the 220-yard high hurdles. He also tied for second in the high jump and ran the anchor leg on the winning Tulare relay team.

Bob Mathias receives advice on how to run the hurdles at the Olympic training grounds in 1952.

At the 1948 California State High School Track Meet at the University of California, Mathias won the low and high hurdles.

Virgil Jackson, Bob's high school coach, decided that the decathlon was best suited to Mathias's talents. He convinced the youngster to try the decathlon, but there was little time to prepare. The 1948 Summer Olympics in London was only a few months away.

Bob was only 17 years old when he began preparing for the 1948 Olympic decathlon. He was familiar with most of the events contested in the decathlon, but he had never attempted a javelin throw or pole vault. Jackson used a track manual to help guide Bob through the techniques of both events.

In order to get Bob some strong competition prior to the Olympics, Jackson entered him in the annual Pacific Coast Games. Bob had practiced only three weeks, but he threw the javelin 171 feet and pole-vaulted 11'6", and he finished first in the decathlon.

At the National Decathlon and Olympics tryout two weeks later, Mathias outpointed three-time national champion Irving Mondschein by a substantial margin to win a place on the U.S. Olympic team.

In London, Bob was pitted against the best athletes from 19 countries. Mathias's inexperience showed on the first day with his performance in the shot put. He threw the 16-pound ball over 45', but an official raised the red flag indicating a foul. Mathias didn't know that it was against the rules to leave the throwing circle from the front. His best throw after that was only 42–9 1/4.

His disappointment in the shot put nearly cost

him in the next event, the high jump. Bob had always performed well in the high jump, but he had trouble concentrating and missed on two attempts at 5–9. Then, in his final attempt, he disregarded the formal technique he had been taught by Jackson and summoned up all his athletic ability. He ran at the bar and just threw his body upward in a clumsy fashion, but the jump was successful. He went on to clear 6–1 1/2 and was in third place at the end of the first five events.

The next day's competition took more than 12 hours to complete because of bad weather. One major delay came during Mathias's discus throw. He got off a throw of about 145' but the marker on his throw got knocked over. Officials searched for half an hour in the rain for the hole left by his discus but could not find it. Eventually they awarded Bob a throw of 144–4. Bob's older brother, Gene, urged him to make the officials keep looking for the hole but Bob felt guilty about the delay he was causing and accepted the officials' ruling. The throw was good enough to put Bob into first place.

At 10:35 p.m., Bob staggered across the finish line in the 1,500 to learn that he had become the decathlon champion and the youngest winner of a men's track and field event in the history of the Olympic Games. Bob won only one event in the decathlon—the pole vault—but he placed so high in many others that he outdistanced runner-up Ignace Henrich of France by 122 points. In the dressing room afterward, the exhausted teenager was asked how he intended to celebrate the victory. "I'll start shaving, I guess," he replied.

Actually Bob didn't celebrate at all. He was so

Mathias clears 13–1.47 in the pole vault, extending his lead during the 1952 Olympics in Helsinki.

tired he went right to bed and had to be awakened to take part in the victory ceremony the next day.

As a result of his Olympic decathlon victory, Bob was besieged with offers to endorse products. But he turned them all down to maintain his amateur status. He hoped to go to college, but months away from his studies had left him unprepared for college entrance exams and he failed to pass.

In order to better prepare himself for college, he enrolled at Kiski School in Salzburg, Pennsylvania. There he became a standout football player and received a scholarship to Stanford University. At Stanford, Bob became a star fullback and led the team to its first conference title in 12 years. Bob participated in Stanford's 1952 Rose Bowl loss to Illinois.

While at Stanford, Bob continued to prepare himself for the 1952 Olympic Games in Helsinki, Finland. He grew bigger and stronger, and his times and distances improved steadily. In 1950, he surpassed a world record in the decathlon that had stood since 1936.

Even though he was better prepared in 1952 than he had been four years earlier, Bob knew that his competition had also improved and that he would face increased pressure. The Soviet Union had entered the Games for the first time in 40 years, and they brought with them not only outstanding athletes but also the intensity of Cold War politics.

No one came close to beating Bob in Helsinki, however. He bettered his previous world mark by 62 points to finish well ahead of American teammates Milt Campbell and Floyd Simmons. He had become the first man ever to win the decathlon twice. It was a record that would stand for 32 years until England's Daley Thompson equaled it by winning Olympic decathlons in 1980 and 1984.

Bob might have had a shot at winning three Olympic decathlons, but he decided to try his luck at acting and was cast as himself in "The Bob Mathias Story." The movie bombed at the box office and ended up costing Bob his amateur status. Because he had been paid for making the movie, the AAU declared him a professional and Bob's athletic career came to an abrupt end. "At the time I was terribly disap-

Milt Campbell, shown here putting the shot at the 1953 AAU national championship, won a gold medal in the decathlon at the 1956 Olympics.

pointed," said Bob. "In 1956, I was still only 25. I was at my peak, still growing as an athlete."

Although he was through with competitive sports, Bob cashed in on his name for many years. He served as a member of the U.S. House of Representatives as a Republican from California's 18th district from 1967 to 1974. He later served as director or president of several other business enterprises.

He rightfully earned his place in history as perhaps the greatest all-around athlete of the 20th century . . . although there was at least one dissenter. "Mathias hasn't had a chance to play as many sports as I did," said Jim Thorpe during a 1951 interview with *Life* magazine. "But even if he had, he probably wouldn't be as good as me."

There were many great decathletes who followed in the footsteps of Mathias. Among them were Milt Campbell, Rafer Johnson, Bruce Jenner, and Dan O'Brien of the United States and England's Daley Thompson.

Rafer Johnson won the gold medal at the 1960 Rome Olympics, defeating his collegiate friend Yang Chuan-Kwang by only 58 points. Johnson had to run a career best 4:49.7 in the final event, the 1,500-meter, to win the title.

Bruce Jenner won the decathlon at the 1976 Olympics in Montreal by setting a world record. The victory enabled him to achieve international fame and made him a millionaire.

Daley Thompson equaled Mathias's achievement by winning back-to-back Olympic decathlons in 1980 in Moscow and 1984 in Los Angeles. However, both Olympics were tainted by boycotts. Several countries, including the United States and West Germany, did not compete in Moscow, and Thompson did not have to compete against Guido Kratschmer of West Germany, considered one of the top decathletes in the world. In Los Angeles, the Soviet Union and other communist countries did not participate, so Thompson was spared having to battle the tough athletes from the U.S.S.R. He won the event easily. Four years later he tried again in Seoul, South Korea, but he injured himself in a pole-vaulting fall and finished fourth.

3

ROGER BANNISTER: THE STANDARD-BEARER

Born in Harrow, England, on March 23, 1929, Roger Bannister was a grammar school student at the City of Bath boys' school when he first became interested in athletics. He did so out of fear of "not belonging" at school unless he commanded respect in sports. He began running at age 11 and was 13 when he won his first footrace, a three-mile junior cross-country race near Bath, England. "As a boy I had no clear understanding of why I wanted to run," he said. "I just ran anywhere—never because it was an end in itself, but because it was easier for me to run than walk."

In 1946, he entered Exeter College at Oxford University to study medicine and decided to take up track. A year earlier, Gundar Haegg, a Swedish runner, had lowered the world record

Roger Bannister breaks the tape to become the first person ever to run a mile in under four minutes. His nearest competitor, Chris Chataway (rear), was 60 yards and over seven seconds behind Bannister.

23

for the mile to 4:01.4 and now it seemed certain that the first sub–four-minute mile was in reach.

Bannister made the Oxford track team in 1947 and earned a place as the team's third-string miler in the Oxford-Cambridge meet. Surprisingly, he won the race with a time of 4:30.8. "I suddenly tapped that hidden source of energy I always suspected I possessed," said Roger. Bannister's times steadily improved, and within 16 months he had reduced his time to 4:17.2. In 1949, he turned in an impressive 4:11.1 mile at a meet in the United States, and by the following year he had reduced his time to 4:09.9.

After graduating from Oxford in 1950, he enrolled at the school for another two years to work toward another degree that was necessary in his bid to become a doctor. He continued to run, and in the spring of 1951 at Franklin Field in Philadelphia he ran the mile in 4:08.3 minutes, breaking a meet record established by Glenn Cunningham 17 years earlier.

Bannister trained far fewer hours than most middle-distance runners. His busy academic schedule allowed him less time to devote to the sport. He also trained alone, without the technical expertise of a coach.

He obtained his Bachelor of Science degree from Oxford in the early summer of 1952 and immediately enrolled at St. Mary's Hospital Medical School in London. He somehow was able to balance his schedule well enough to make the British Olympic team.

At the Olympics, Bannister was clearly not in top shape. The competitors had to race three times in three days in order to qualify for the 1,500-meter final. In the final, Roger finished a disappointing fourth, sixth-tenths of a second away from a medal.

Aware that his medical studies would prevent him from competing at any future Olympics, Bannister returned from Helsinki with his mind set on leaving his mark on the sport. He would devote himself to breaking the four-minute mile.

In order to increase his endurance, he began practicing a series of endurance exercises suggested by Dr. Thomas Kirk Cureton Jr. of the University of Illinois. He also did not compete for almost a year.

When he did return, he was in far better condition. On May 2, 1953, at the Iffley Road track at Oxford, he ran the mile in 4:03.6 minutes, officially breaking the British national record. Six weeks later, at an invitational meet at Motspur Park in Surrey, he lowered that time to 4:02, the third-fastest time ever recorded, and only 0.6 seconds over the world record established by Haegg in 1945.

"I think Bannister is the man to beat four minutes," said Haegg in early 1954. "He uses his brains as much as his legs. I've always thought the four-minute mile more of a psychological problem than a test of physical endurance."

Roger set May 6, 1954, as the target date for breaking the four-minute barrier. On that date, an All-Star team was scheduled to meet Bannister's Oxford club at Oxford. "I approached this race with the thought that this is the only chance I would have—there must be no letup," said Roger.

He knew that if he failed to achieve his goal in this meet, he probably would not be the first to crack the four-minute mark. Other runners, such as John Landy of Australia and Wes Santee of the United States, were also closing in on the mark.

"I tried to establish this now-or-never attitude because I knew that unless I was successful in attaining this attitude or mental stance, I would perhaps spoil my attempt by letting myself fall prey to the mental reaction so common to athletes: that this would not be 'one of those days' when things became difficult and muscles began to ache from the strain," said Bannister.

On the morning of May 6, Roger almost changed his mind about going for the record because of a stiff breeze. But the wind dropped by the time the race was to start and Roger decided to give his best effort. He started off well, covering the first lap in 57.5 seconds. At the halfway mark, his time was 1:58. The crowd was roaring its approval on every step he took, but Roger knew he would have to stay relaxed if he was going to continue with that pace. At the three-quarters mark, his time was 3:00.7.

Drawing on all his physical strength and mental concentration, he pushed himself to the limit. He sprinted down the straightaway and was in a daze as he crossed the finish line. He nearly passed out and had to be helped from the track by teammates. As the official timekeeper began with the words, "three minutes . . ." the crowd began cheering wildly. They never heard the exact official time of 3:59.4. They knew that Roger had done what no man had ever done.

Roger's name filled newspaper headlines around the globe.

Less than two months later, John Landy broke Roger's record by a full second. Then the two were entered in the British Commonwealth

Games at Vancouver, British Columbia, on August 7, 1954. Roger knew that he was going to have to beat Landy in order to prove that his performance in breaking the four-minute barrier was no fluke.

Landy decided to run as fast as he could for the first three-quarters of the race. That way Roger would be so tired in trying to keep up that he would have nothing left at the end. Or so Landy thought.

Landy was ahead at the halfway mark in a time of 1:58. The other runners in the race faded far to the rear. Roger began to make his move 200 yards from the finish line. With 90 yards to go, he lengthened his stride and slowly pulled ahead of Landy. He crossed the finish line in 3:58.8 to the roar of the crowd and fell into the arms of the English team manager. Landy finished eight-tenths of a second later and assisted in helping the exhausted Roger off the track. Two men had bettered the four-minute mile in

After the race in which he broke the four-minute mark, Bannister embraces his competitors Chris Brasher (left) and Chris Chataway. Chataway, who finished second, set a personal best of 4:07.2 in the race.

*In 1966, Jim Ryun set a new
record for the mile: 3:51.3.*

the same race for the first time in history.

"I tried to pull away from him in the backstretch of the last lap," said Landy after the race. "I had hoped that the pace would be so fast that he would crack at that point. He didn't. When you get a man in that sort of a situation and he doesn't crack, you do."

Three weeks later Roger won his last international track meet. He took the 1,500 meters in the European Games in Bern, Switzerland. In December 1954, he retired from international competition to devote himself full-time to his medical practice. He received numerous honors from the British government and became one of the country's most respected physicians.

Roger Bannister's achievement inspired many youngsters to become middle-distance runners. In the years following his breaking of the four-minute mile, training methods and track conditions improved so much that the mile record was lowered considerably with each passing year.

Jim Ryun, a native of Wichita, Kansas, broke the four-minute barrier when he was in high school, becoming the youngest ever to achieve that feat. Although he never won an Olympic gold medal, he lowered the world record in the mile twice and also held the 1,500-meter record. **Peter Snell** of New Zealand was Ryun's toughest rival during the 1960s and 1970s. He twice broke the mile record and won the gold medal in the 1,500 meters in the 1964 Olympics. He also was the 800-meter gold medalist in 1960 and 1964.

Kip Keino, a Kenyan, was the gold medalist in the 1,500 meters at the 1968 Olympics and won the gold medal in the steeplechase at the 1972 Olympics.

Next to Bannister, **Sebastian Coe** was England's most famous middle-distance runner. He was a gold medalist in the 1,500 meters and silver medalist in the 800 meters at the 1980 and 1984 Olympics. In 1981, he set the 800-meter world record when he ran 1:41.73. He was elected to the British Parliament in 1992.

Said Aouita of Morocco once held the world record for the 1,500 meters but is more well-known for his performances in the 5,000 meters. He was the first man to run the 5,000 meters in less than 13 minutes. He won the gold medal in the 5,000 meters at the 1984 Olympics.

Noureddine Morceli of Algeria is the only miler in the world to be ranked No. 1 for four consecutive years. In 1993, he was undefeated and he shattered the eight-year-old outdoor mile record by running 3:44.39. He also holds both the indoor and outdoor world records for the 1,500 meters.

4

AL OERTER: THE CONSUMMATE COMPETITOR

Born on September. 19, 1936, in West Babylon, New York, Alfred A. Oerter became interested in throwing the discus while in his teens, and he reached national prominence by setting the national high school record. His skill earned him a scholarship to the University of Kansas, and he showed signs of becoming a star in the sport. The only thing he lacked was experience.

In 1956, at the age of 20, Al made the U.S. Olympic team, even though he had finished only fourth in the National Collegiate Athletic Association (NCAA) meet and sixth in the Amateur Athletic Association meet. He was 6'3" and 220 pounds, but most of the competitors he would be facing at the Summer Games in Melbourne, Australia, were much older and more established. Among the competitors were 39-year-old Adolfo Consolini of Italy, the 1948 Olympic champion and 1952 silver medalist, and two-time

Al Oerter, shown here at age 46, was the greatest discus thrower of all time.

Olympic veteran Ferenc Klics of Hungary. Al also had to contend with teammate Fortune Gordien, 34, a bronze medalist at the 1948 Olympics and the world record holder in the event.

On the day of the competition, Al was keyed up and inspired. He watched as Consolini, Klics, and Gordien each fell short of their personal bests on the first round. When Al's turn came he let loose the best throw of his career— 184–11. "I don't know how I ever did it, but everything just came out right," Al said.

Al had the best throws in the next two rounds as well, and none of his competitors was within five feet of him. On the victory stand he suddenly realized that he had actually won. His knees buckled and he almost fell.

A year after the Olympics, Al was involved in a near-fatal car crash. He recovered completely and was soon back in top shape. Over the next few years Al continued to improve, and his reputation for winning big meets improved as he posted victories in the NCAA, AAU, and Pan American championships.

At the 1960 U.S. Olympic trials, Al suffered his first defeat in over two years when he lost to Rink Babka, a powerfully built man who towered over everyone. Babka had thrown over 200' during the year, far better than Al's best toss. Still, Al entered the Olympic Games in Rome as the slight favorite.

While warming up for the qualifying round, he casually threw the discus beyond the world record marker and then qualified with an Olympic record of 191–8. But on the day of the final, Al was extremely tense.

Babka led off and tossed the discus 190–4. Al had hoped to put his best effort into his first toss, but his foot slipped and he could manage only 189–1. He threw even shorter on his second try and still less on his third throw. He improved slightly on his fourth attempt, but Babka's first toss was still good enough for the lead.

As Al prepared for his fifth and final toss, Babka told him that he seemed to be doing something wrong with his left arm. Al made a small adjustment in his delivery and tossed the discus 194–2, the best throw of his life. He walked over and thanked Babka for the advice, then wished him luck on his final toss. Babka's toss was short, however, and Al had won his second gold medal.

With his weight now up to 260 pounds, on May 18, 1962, Al became the first discus thrower to officially break the 200-foot barrier, with a throw of 200–5. Two more times Al boosted the record until he got to 205–5 1/2.

Al was not healthy as he prepared for his third Olympics in Tokyo, Japan. He had been suffering for quite some time from a chronic cervical disc injury, which caused him to wear a neck harness. In addition, he had torn the cartilage in his ribs while practicing in Tokyo less than a week before the competition. He was advised by doctors to rest for six weeks, but he did not listen to them. On the day of the preliminary round he got a shot of novacaine and wrapped his ribs with ice packs and tape to prevent internal bleeding.

On the first day of the competition, Al told a friend, "If I don't do it on the first throw, I won't be able to do it at all." In qualifying, Al set an Olympic record with a throw of 198–8. However, in the finals, his first attempt only went 189–1. His chief competitor, Ludvik Danek, a Czech who had won 45 consecutive competitions, took the lead on his first throw and continued to hold it after four rounds.

Al was in third place after four rounds and had only one more chance to take the gold medal. He decided to give it all he had. As he let go of the discus, he doubled over in pain. But he had gotten off a strong throw, and when the discus landed Al had become the first person in Olympic history to surpass 200 feet. His throw of 200-1 set another Olympic record and earned a third gold medal.

A try for a fourth gold medal in 1968 seemed out of the question. Al was long out of college and was married with a family. He was well into a successful data-processing career at an aircraft plant. But the excitement of competition was too much for him to pass up. Still, he knew he couldn't devote as much time to training as he had in the past. So, he decided to organize his practices better. He would train harder but for shorter periods of time.

Once again he qualified for the Olympic team, and his main nemesis this time was a fellow teammate, Jay Silvester. Silvester was the world record holder and had thrown over 224 feet. Al's best throw in 1968 had been 205-10. Even Al didn't think he had much of a chance to win.

Silvester got off a toss of 207-10 in the preliminary round, which was well short of his world record but still two inches better than Al had ever done.

Al needed some divine intervention if he was to succeed in winning the gold medal. He got it. The final round was delayed by rain for an hour, and this seemed to upset Silvester. When the competition finally got under way, Lothar Milde

Oerter won his second gold medal at the 1960 Olympics. He also took home the gold in 1964 and 1968.

of East Germany took the first round lead with a throw of 204-10. He improved that to 206-11 with his second attempt.

As the third round began, Al stood in fourth place behind Milde, Hartmuth Losch of East Germany, and Silvester. Al then unleashed a throw of 212-6, five feet farther than he had ever thrown before, and grabbed the lead. The rest of the competitors were demoralized, especially Silvester, who fouled on his next three attempts. Al added throws of 212-5 and 210-1, and nobody came close to beating his 212-6. He became the first athlete to win four gold medals in the same event.

Al had now thrown the discus 33,000 times in competition. Although he had once said that he would like to win five gold medals, personal commitments forced him to retire. In 1980, Al decided he would come out of retirement at the age of 43 and try out for the U.S. Olympic team that would compete at the Moscow Olympics. But the United States boycotted the Games.

The discus competition, in which Al Oerter competed, is one of eight events that make up the field events of a track and field competition. The others are the high jump, long jump, triple jump, pole vault, javelin, shot put, and hammer throw.

Charley Dumas of the United States owns the distinction of being the first high jumper ever to clear the 7-foot barrier. He did it on June 29, 1956, at the age of 19. Charley also claimed the gold medal in the 1956 Olympics.

John Thomas and **Valery Brumel** had some of the greatest duels in the history of high jumping. Thomas, an American, cleared the 7-foot barrier more than 30 times in his career and went undefeated for more than two years during the late 1950s and early 1960s. He won a silver medal in both the 1960 and 1964 Olympic Games. Brumel, from Siberia, won a silver medal at the 1960 Olympics and took the gold at the 1964 Summer Games. His career ended abruptly at the age of 23 when he was injured in a motorcycling accident.

Dick Fosbury of the United States revolutionized high jumping with a backwards technique that became known as the "Fosbury Flop." Fosbury's technique began by racing up to the bar at great speed and taking off with the left foot. But instead of swinging his right foot up and over the bar, as everyone else did, he would pivot his right leg back and approach headfirst with his back to the bar. He won the gold medal with this technique at the 1968 Olympics, and by 1980, 13 of the 16 Olympic finalists were using the Fosbury Flop.

The most popular high jumper in American history was probably **Dwight Stones**. A colorful, outspoken person who had a knack for getting the crowd involved in his performance, Stones set the world record numerous times during the 1970s and won bronze medals at the 1972 and 1976 Olympics.

Javier Sotomayor of Cuba was the first to clear eight feet in the high jump, achieving that feat in 1989. He is the only high jumper ever to win an Olympic gold medal twice (1992 and 1996). He established a world record of 8–1/2 inch on July 27, 1993.

Bob Richards was an ordained minister and theology professor in California . . . and the best pole-vaulter of his era. Known as "The Vaulting Vicar," Richards is the only pole-vaulter to win the gold medal at successive Olympics (1952 and 1956). He was ranked No. 1 in the world for eight straight years (1949-56.)

Sergei Bubka of the Ukraine was the first pole-vaulter to clear 20 feet, both indoors and outdoors. He was the gold medalist at the 1988 Olympics. Although Bubka dominated the sport for more than a decade, he failed to earn a medal at either the 1992 or 1996 Olympics.

Jan Zelezny of the Czech Republic set the world record for the javelin throw with a throw of 313 feet, 10 inches in 1993 and also won the gold medal at the 1992 Barcelona Olympics.

5

EDWIN MOSES: A DECADE OF DOMINATION

The son of two educators, Edwin Moses used his brain as much as his physical ability to rule his sport. Born in Dayton, Ohio, on August 31, 1955, Ed grew up in a household where education was stressed before anything else. He showed an early interest in science, art, and music in addition to sports. He first became interested in track in the third grade when he was taken to the Dayton Relays. Because he was small for his age, he was discouraged from playing basketball and baseball, so track became his passion.

Because of racial tensions at Dunbar High School in Dayton, Ed's parents decided to send him to Fairview High School, which was four miles away. There he was one of a few black students among an enrollment of 800. Ed ran track as an extracurricular activity but did not display much of the enormous talent he would in

Edwin Moses races to the gold in the 400-meter hurdles at the 1984 Olympics.

years to come. He did distinguish himself, however, in the classroom, especially in science. His grades were good enough to earn him an academic scholarship to Morehouse College.

Sports were not a big deal at Morehouse. Academics were. The school had a track program, but there were no facilities. Ed trained on his own with a fellow student, a hurdler named Steven Price. It was not until his senior year that he began to take running seriously enough to set his sights on the 1976 Olympics at Montreal.

It was the Florida Relays in Gainesville in March 1976 that Ed considers the turning point of his athletic career. He did not win any races that day, but he posted an impressive 13.7 seconds in the high hurdles, a second place 46.1 in the 400, and a second place 50.1 in the intermediate hurdles. Clearly he had exceptional talent. He just needed someone to help harness it.

Leroy Walker, who would coach the Olympic track and field team that summer, witnessed Ed's performance at Gainesville and immediately saw a star in the making. "Anyone who knew anything about hurdling could see that if they were pointing this guy to something other than the 400 intermediates, they had the wrong race," said Walker. "His size and speed; his base, the ability to carry the stride; his 'skim,' what we call the measurement of the stride over the hurdle—he had it all."

Walker selected Ed to be part of the Olympic development team for that summer's Games. He worked him hard and was impressed with Ed's technique and physical conditioning.

"As we watched him that spring, analyzed his races and charted his progress, Moses perceived the minute techniques of the event so clearly.

He believed in the race. And endurance! He could run the drills we gave him, a 400 flat, then into the lane for a 200 over hurdles . . . Why, he did that last 200 in 25 seconds. Most guys couldn't carry that over a flat! It was obvious nobody would handle him in Montreal. I went to Europe and told them, 'You're all running for second place.'"

One of the things that impressed coaches most about Ed was his ability to take 13 steps between hurdles and maintain that pace throughout the race. Most hurdlers had to take more than that. Andre Phillips was the only other hurdler to attempt a sustained pace of 13 steps between hurdles, and he succeeded only twice.

Although Walker was confident that Ed would be the man to beat at the Montreal Olympics, things did not start well in the spring of 1976. At the NCAA Division III championships in Chicago, a driving rain fogged Ed's glasses. He fell and lost. One month later at an Amateur Athletic Association meet in Los Angeles he finished fourth despite several stumbles.

"I wasn't worried," he said about the mishaps. "I knew how fast I could run. I hit those sticks and broke down and still went under 50. With no mistakes I'm gone."

Ed finally put everything together for the Olympic trials and set an American record of 48.30. But the Olympics were to be his first international meet. How would he fare against the best in the world? The answer: better than anyone else had ever done in an Olympics. He posted a world record time of 47.64 and won the event by eight meters, the largest winning margin in the history of the event.

Unfortunately, the event was deprived of a

potential classic showdown between Moses and the former world record holder John Akii-Bua of Uganda. Akii-Bua was the gold medalist in the 1972 Olympics, but Africa boycotted the '76 Games and Ed was faced with little competition.

Montreal made Ed an instant star on the track and field circuit, and he developed an aura about him, too. Because his eyes were sensitive to light, he always raced in prescription sunglasses, which gave him a sinister appearance. He was also studious, preferring books to interaction with people. So few got to know the real Edwin Moses in his early years.

"I know it was difficult to relate to me back then," he said. "I was black, studying physics and engineering. I was from a small school nobody ever heard of. A guy who took up this race and four months later won the gold medal. All this was fantasy. Then the sunglasses. And they wanted to make me more of a fantasy. But did anybody stop to ask if the sunglasses were prescription? My eyes have been sensitive to light since the fifth grade. Without glasses I can't see the next hurdle."

In June 1977 Ed lowered that world record in the 400 hurdles to 47.45. Two months later, he suffered only the third loss of his career in a meet in Berlin, losing to Harald Schmid, a West German. It was the last loss he would endure for nine years, nine months, and nine days. He began a streak of 122 consecutive victories in September 1977 when he raced 47.58 in the World Cup at Dusseldorf, West Germany.

Ed lowered his own world record to 47.13 in a meet in Milan, Italy, in July 1980 and was ready to successfully defend his Olympic gold medal at the 1980 Moscow Olympics. But this

At the 1976 Olympics, Moses set a world record in winning the 400-meter hurdles. At left is fellow American Michael Shine, who won the silver medal.

time it was the United States that boycotted the event. U.S. President Jimmy Carter called for an American boycott of the Olympics as a protest of the Soviet invasion of Afghanistan.

In August 1983, Ed once again broke his own world record in the 400 meters with a time of 47.02 at Koblenz, West Germany. Later that year he received the prestigious Sullivan Award, given annually to the best American amateur athlete.

One year later he was back in the Olympics . . . and this time with an added responsibility. He was chosen by the U.S. Olympic team to recite the Olympic oath on behalf of all the participants at the opening ceremonies of the Games in Los Angeles.

Moses won his second Olympic gold medal easily, with a time of 47.75 in the 400 hurdles.

*Renaldo Nehemiah wins the
110-meter hurdles at the
1979 World Cup. Nehemiah
was one of the first
world-class track stars to
take up professional football.*

Ed's only regret was that he didn't get to race against some of the best athletes. Another boycott, this one by the Soviet Union and other communist countries, kept a number of top hurdlers out of the competition.

After Los Angeles, Ed kept right on winning. As his winning streak grew he became more famous. He became chairman of the United States Olympic Committee's committee on substance abuse. He was making a half million dollars a year from endorsements and track promoters, who would pay him $20,000 for an appearance.

Ed's winning streak finally ended on June 4, 1987, when he was beaten by only .13 of a second by Danny Harris, the silver medalist at the Los Angeles Olympics.

"I wasn't disappointed. It was just destiny," said Ed. "The streak was made concrete by the loss. I went right back to my training program."

Although he was 33 years old at the time, Ed won 10 more 400 hurdles races in a row and qualified for the 1988 Seoul Olympics. He was favored to win the race but finished third for the bronze medal. His reign of domination was over.

Edwin Moses left an indelible mark on the sport of hurdling. Those who watched him perform were left mesmerized by his exquisite form.

"Compared to Ed, everyone else looked like roosters with their tails on fire," said hurdling coach Dick Hill of Southern University.

Of course, there were other great hurdlers before Edwin Moses. **Alvin Kraenzlein**, a student at the University of Pennsylvania in the 1890s, revolutionized hurdling by introducing the style that is used today—extending one leg ahead over the hurdles instead of jumping over with both legs tucked up as most competitors did then. Kraenzlein won four gold medals at the 1900 Olympics, including victories in the 110- and 200-meter hurdles.

Rod Milburn won 27 consecutive finals yet almost didn't qualify for the 1972 Munich Olympics when he hit two hurdles at the U.S. Olympic trials and barely qualified in third place. However, when he participated in Munich he won the race easily.

Willie Davenport competed in three Olympics as a hurdler for the United States. He won the gold medal at the 1968 Mexico City Olympics and took a bronze in the 1976 Games after finishing fourth in 1972. Davenport also competed in the 1980 Winter Olympics as a member of the U.S. bobsled team.

Renaldo Nehemiah was the first to run the 110-meter hurdles in under 13 seconds. He dominated the sport from the late 1970s through the early 1980s.

Glenn Davis, not to be confused with the Army football star of the same name, won gold medals in the 400-meter hurdles at the 1956 and 1960 Olympic Games. He was the first person to break the 50-second barrier in the 400 hurdles.

6

CARL LEWIS: THE BEST OF ALL TIME

It all began for Carl at the Willingboro Track Club in Willingboro, New Jersey. Carl's father, Bill Lewis, had been a football star at Tuskegee Institute in Alabama, and his mother, Evelyn, also a Tuskegee graduate, had represented the United States at the Pan American Games in 1951.

Both of them were schoolteachers but their passion was track. Carl was born on July 1, 1961, in Birmingham, Alabama, but the family moved to Willingboro when Carl was very young. The family was heavily into sports. Carl's oldest brother, Mack, was a high school sprinter, and Cleve, the next oldest, played professional soccer. His younger sister, Carol, competed in the Olympics as a long jumper and also was an outstanding sprinter, hurdler, and high jumper.

Carl, who now stands 6'2" and weighs 180 pounds, was small as a child. So small that Carol

Carl Lewis anchored the 4 x 100-meter relay to a world record and gold medal at the 1992 World Championship.

47

used to beat him regularly at track events. "I didn't mature until high school while others began maturing in seventh, eighth grade," recalled Carl. "There was talent there all the time, but it was only when I got older that I really blossomed."

Carl began running for his parents' track club when he was eight years old. When he was 12, he won the long jump at a Jesse Owens Youth Program meet in Philadelphia with a leap of 17–6, even though he was much smaller than the other competitors.

Between his sophomore and junior years in high school Carl began to grow rapidly. He could jump more than 22 feet by his sophomore year, and by his junior year he had increased his distance to more than 25 feet. In the 1978 national junior championships in Memphis, Tennessee, he ran the 100-yard dash in 9.3 seconds and long jumped 25-9, a national high school record.

In his senior year at Willingboro, Carl was the best in the nation in the 200 meters and the long jump. He was the top-ranked high school track athlete in the United States.

Carl's success earned him an athletic scholarship to the University of Houston, and there he came under the guidance of Tom Tellez, one of the most respected track and field coaches in the country.

Carl qualified for the 1980 Moscow Olympics but never got a chance to compete for the gold medal that year because the United States boycotted the Games in protest of the Soviet Union's invasion of Afghanistan. That winter Carl turned to the indoor track and field circuit and began to make a name for himself.

He won the 100-meter dash and the long jump

at the NCAA's indoor championships in the spring of 1981, becoming the first athlete in the history of the event to finish first in both a track and a field event. Two weeks later he repeated his double at the U.S. outdoor track and field championships in Sacramento, California. At the end of the year he was named winner of the Sullivan Award by the Amateur Athletic Union as the best amateur athlete of 1981.

At the national outdoor championships in Knoxville, Tennessee, in 1982, Carl achieved his third major double.

Unfortunately, Carl was not applying himself in the classroom as hard as he was on the track. His grades were not good enough for him to participate in track and field for the University of Houston in the 1981-82 season, so he competed for the Santa Monica (California) Track Club.

In 1983, Carl began preparing for the 1984 Olympics, which were going to be on American soil in Los Angeles. He competed in the Athletics Congress outdoor championships in Indianapolis and turned in his most memorable performance to date by winning three events. He captured the long jump with a leap of 28-10, won the 100 meters in 10.27, and took the 200 meters in 19.75, just .03 seconds off the world record set by Italy's Pietro Minnea. Many observers felt that Carl would have broken the record had he not raised his arms in a victory salute before crossing the finish line. Carl had long come under criticism from his rivals for "showboating" tactics, and they pointed to this gesture as a perfect example.

At the 1983 world championships at Helsinki, Finland, Carl won three gold medals, taking the 100 meters and the long jump and anchoring the world record-setting 4 x 100-meter relay team. Carl ran his leg of the race in an astounding 8.9 seconds.

Because he had become so dominant in his events, reports began circulating that he was taking illegal muscle-building drugs to enhance his performance. Carl, wanting to show young people that drugs were not necessary to improve performance, agreed to be tested and was found to be clean.

Carl finally reached superstardom at the 1984 Olympics. He won the 100-meter dash, the 200 meters, and the long jump, and he anchored the winning 4 x 100-meter relay team. His four gold medals equaled Jesse Owens' total from the 1936 Games.

Unlike Owens, however, Carl failed to become a national hero. Instead, the crowd turned on him in the long jump for his refusal to attempt a world record. He jumped 28-7 on his first attempt, fouled on his next, then passed on his next four jumps. While his 28-7 held up for first place, the fans were angry with Carl for not going after the record.

"I got a little sore after the second jump and didn't want to risk a chance at injury," Carl explained.

Following the Olympics, Carl competed in five European countries, pleasing crowds there more than he had at the Olympics. However, he did not do as well financially from the four gold medals as had been expected. The people had judged him as "arrogant" for his refusal to go for a world record in the long jump at Los Angeles, and advertisers stayed away from him. It took four years for Carl to earn back a measure of

For nine years, no one could beat Carl Lewis in the long jump. This jump of 27'6" won the gold medal at the 1990 Goodwill Games.

respect from the American public . . . and it came in a race in which he finished a distant second. At the 1988 Seoul Olympics, a fierce battle for the gold medal was expected between Carl and Canada's Ben Johnson. However, the race wasn't close. Johnson broke from the blocks like a racehorse and won the race handily while Carl had to settle for the silver medal. Two days later, however, it was revealed that Johnson had tested positive for steroids, a muscle builder, and the Canadian was disqualified. Carl was awarded the gold medal.

Carl was very gracious in a difficult situation. "I feel very sad for Ben and for the Canadian public," he said. "You can talk track up to a certain point. After that you talk people. Imagine the burden on Ben. Imagine what his family will go through."

Carl's gentlemanly conduct won back the hearts of many Americans, and when he picked up another gold medal in the long jump he added to his growing legend.

Carl had been busy taking acting and singing lessons for several years and had told friends that he someday hoped to be a respected entertainer. But the thrill of competing was still too great in him, and he found it impossible to step down even though he was nearly 30 years old.

At the 1991 world championships in Tokyo, he lost in his specialty, the long jump, to Mike Powell of the United States, but he amazed even himself by setting a world record in the 100 meters.

Carl regained his title as the world's best long jumper by winning the gold medal at the 1992 Barcelona Olympics, and he added another gold medal as the anchor on the 4 x 100-meter relay team, which established a world record.

By 1993, however, his days as a world-class sprinter were ending. He entered the World Championships in Stuttgart, Germany, with hopes of adding to his collection of 16 World Championship or Olympic gold medals. But the best he could do was a bronze medal in the 200 meters. He did not enter the long jump competition because of a chronic back problem.

Injuries were now becoming more frequent. An injured leg prevented Carl from competing in the 1995 World Championships in Gotheburg, Sweden, and he did not qualify for the 1996 U.S. Olympic team in the sprints. He did, however, manage to make the U.S. team in the long jump.

The 1996 Olympics were being held in Atlanta, Georgia, and Carl knew it would be his last one. He wanted to go out a winner on his home turf. No one gave Carl much chance to win another gold medal, but in one of the most dramatic moments in Olympic history, Carl won the competition on his final jump. It was his ninth Olympic gold medal, tying him with legendary Finnish runner Paavo Nurmi for the most in history. It was also the fourth Olympics in a row that he had won the long jump competition, tying discus thrower Al Oerter's record of having won the same event in four straight Olympics.

Carl wanted a chance at a record 10th gold medal and hoped to get added to the 4 x 100 relay team, even though he had not qualified among the fastest runners. Four years before in Barcelona, Carl had been added to the relay team to run anchor, even though his time had been sixth fastest at the trials, and the team set a world record. But this time the coach refused to bow to public pressure and did not put Carl on the team. The United States lost to Canada.

Oddly, a similar thing had happened to Nurmi. In search of his 10th gold medal in 1924, he was pulled out of the lineup by the Finnish coach so that another teammate might have a chance at the gold medal. That runner, Vilho Ritola, won the event in world record time. Back in Finland after the Games, Nurmi ran the race 17 seconds faster than Ritola.

As with Nurmi, the one thing track and field fans will remember most about Carl Lewis is his competitive spirit. The fact he won the long jump at the age of 35 on his last jump did not surprise those who followed his career.

Bob Beaman's long jump of 29–2.5 at the 1968 Olympics in Mexico City shattered the record. It took more than 25 years before anyone jumped that distance again.

"I'm going to leave this sport on top," he said shortly before the Olympics. "It's going to be on my terms. I've earned that right."

Carl Lewis and Jesse Owens are the only two athletes ever to win Olympic gold medals in both sprints and long jumping. But another notable athlete who starred in both disciplines was **Eulace Peacock**. In 1935, the year before Owens won four gold medals at the Berlin Olympics, Peacock defeated Owens in seven of 10 meetings. However, injury prevented him from making the 1936 Olympic team, and he did not get to compete in 1940 or 1944 because both of those Olympics were canceled due to World War II.

Other standout long jumpers in Olympic history were **Ralph Boston** and **Bob Beamon**. Boston broke Owens's world record in 1960 with a leap of 26–11 1/4. He went on to win a gold medal at the 1960 Olympics, a silver at the 1964 Games, and a bronze at the 1968 Games. Boston was ranked No. 1 in the world from 1960 to 1967.

Beamon earned international acclaim for his world record–setting leap of 29–1 1/2 at the 1968 Olympics in Mexico City. Beamon's achievement was hailed as the greatest athletic achievement of all time by many track and field followers. His record stood until 1991, when Mike Powell of the United States broke it with a leap of 29-4 1/2.

The triple jump, which used to be called the hop, step, and jump, differs from the long jump in that the competitors land on the same foot with which they take off, take one step onto the other foot, and then jump. If their trailing foot touches the ground, the jump is ruled a foul. **Viktor Saneyev** of the former Soviet republic of Georgia is the most dominant competitor in the history of the event. He won gold medals in three straight Olympics (1968, 1972, and 1976) and was ranked No. 1 in the world for nine consecutive years (1968-76).

Eddie Tolan, Bobby Morrow, and **Valery Borzov** also had something in common with Owens and Lewis: they were double winners of the 100- and 200-meter events in an Olympic Games. Tolan won both events in 1932, Morrow in 1956, and Borzov in 1972.

7

MICHAEL JOHNSON: FASTEST MAN ON EARTH

Although Michael Johnson could run faster than any kid on the block in his hometown of Dallas, Texas, he didn't feel any particular passion for racing as a youngster. In fact, he didn't look like much of an athlete, with his neat appearance, eyeglasses, and penchant for carrying a briefcase to school.

In his first race at Atwell Junior High, he placed second in the 200. But his parents insisted that academics come before sports, and Michael did not pursue track very diligently. In fact, he took a few years off to concentrate on his studies. His mother, Ruby, was a schoolteacher and she would tutor her four children every day during the summer vacations to prepare them for the next school year.

It was not until his junior year at Skyline High School in Dallas that he returned to competitive running. He ran differently from most, with an

Michael Johnson was considered the fastest man in the world in the late 1990s.

erect style that his coach, Joel Ezar, said made him look like "a statue."

"They say his feet never leave the ground," said Ezar.

Still, Michael was good enough to finish second in the 200 at the Texas State Meet. But his time of 21.30 did not attract very many scholarship offers.

One of those who was interested was Clyde Hart, head coach at Baylor University. Hart had coached some of the best mile relay teams in the nation during his years at Baylor, and he recruited Michael as a potential member of the relay team. Hart wanted to change Michael's running style but he resisted the temptation. It was a good thing, too, because Michael shocked Hart by setting a school record of 20.41 in the 200 in his first collegiate meet. A year later he was being hailed by Hart as a possible world-record setter in both the 200 and 400.

Injuries, however, were to slow Michael's progress. He broke his leg in the 200 final at the NCAA championships in 1988, and a pulled hamstring prevented him making the finals at both the NCAA and USA meets in 1989.

Finally free from injury, Michael developed into the No. 1-ranked sprinter in the world in both the 200 and 400 in 1990. It marked the first time that any sprinter had been ranked first in both events.

In 1991, Michael went undefeated at both distances. Unable to compete in both events at the 1991 World Championships because of a scheduling conflict, Michael chose the 200 and won the gold medal in an impressive time of 20.01 against a stiff head wind.

Once again a scheduling conflict prevented

Michael from entering both events at the 1992 Barcelona Olympics. But he entered the Games as the overwhelming favorite to win the 200 meters. However, he suffered a bad case of food poisoning and failed to qualify for the final. He broke down in tears following the race, but the loving support of his parents helped him overcome the bitter disappointment. Michael decided to stick around for the 4 x 400-meter relay and he was glad he did. He ran the anchor leg and helped the United States to the gold medal in world-record time.

The following year Michael concentrated on the 400 and also tried his hand at the 100. He broke the 44-second barrier three times in the 400 and won both the USA title and the World Championships. He also anchored the victorious 4 x 400 relay team at the World Championships to a world record while turning in the fastest relay leg in history (42.94).

In 1994, Michael decided that he wanted to become the first sprinter in history to break the 10.00, 20.00, and 44.00 barriers. He began working harder at the 100, but he pulled up lame in the 100 final of the USA meet. After his recovery he switched back to his two specialties and went undefeated after mid-July. For his efforts he won the coveted Jesse Owens Award.

He received that award again in 1995 after his unprecedented double at the World Championships in Goteborg, Sweden, and he was named Sportsman of the Year by the U.S. Olympic Committee.

Michael knew that he could repeat his double at the Atlanta Olympics if he could get the IAAF to change the schedule. The original schedule had two days on which both the 200m and 400m

*Michael Johnson shows off
the prize for winning a world
championship: a gold medal.*

would be contested.

"If the schedule is right, I am the only person who can stop me from getting three medals," Michael said.

He appealed to Primo Nebiolo, the president of the IAAF, but Nebiolo resisted at first before finally giving in. Nebiolo got the International Olympic Committee to change the schedule so that there was a full day's rest between the final of the 400m and the first-round heats of the

200m.

The decision to change the race times just about destroyed the morale of the other competitors in the 400m. Britain's Roger Black said before the 400m that no one had a chance to beat Michael in the race, and he proved to be right.

Running in handmade golden spikes, Michael won the race by almost a full second over Black. "The only way to beat Michael is to run a perfect race and have him make a mistake," said Black. "But he doesn't make mistakes."

Michael knew his task would be tougher in the 200m. While he was clearly superior to the competition in the 400m, this was not the case in the 200m. Jamaica's Frank Fredericks had beaten Michael three times at this distance.

Both men performed well in the qualifying heats, with Fredericks turning in an impressive 19.98 in the semifinals. In the final, the two men raced neck and neck into the stretch. Then, with about 90 meters to go, Michael went into another gear and pulled away from Fredericks. When he crossed the finish line he had set a world record of 19.32, and the partisan U.S. crowd erupted in thunderous praise.

"Anywhere else I might have run 19.5 or 19.6," Michael said. "But the crowd here was unbelievable. They were a big part of this. I never before heard an explosion like that when I crossed the line."

Hart was stunned by Michael's achievement.

"When Babe Ruth pointed to center field and said he was going to hit a home run, very few people really realized what that meant, in physical terms," said Hart. "Yet he did it and the story grew into legend.

"But Michael told a billion people, 'Change the [Olympic] schedule. I'm going to do the double. I'm going to be the show in Atlanta.' And he pulled it off. That's scary. I told Michael, 'You like that pressure. I don't know if I do.'"

Unfortunately, Michael injured his hamstring slightly in the race and could not participate in the 4 x 400 relay. Still, his achievement at Atlanta earned him Male Athlete of the Year honors by the Associated Press.

Michael's achievement may be duplicated in the future, and athletes may run the races faster. But he will always have the satisfaction of knowing that he was the first.

There have been many outstanding performances in the 200 and 400m but few athletes have excelled at both distances. Scotland's **Eric Liddell**, immortalized in the Academy Award winning movie "Chariots of Fire," was one who did achieve fame in both events. Liddell finished third in the 200m and won a gold medal in the 400m at the 1924 Olympic Games.

An unusual Olympic track double victory was also posted in 1976 by Cuba's **Alberto Juantorena**. He won both the 400 and 800 meters, becoming the first man since **Paul Pilgrim** in the 1906 Intercalated Games to achieve that rare double.

There are several athletes who have won both the 100 and 200m events in a single Olympics. They include **Archie Hahn** (1902), **Eddie Tolan** (1932), **Jesse Owens** (1936), **Bobby Morrow** (1956), **Valery Borzov** (1972), and **Carl Lewis** (1984).

FURTHER READING

Bannister, Roger. *The Four Minute Mile*. New York: Dodd, Mead, 1981.

Johnson, Michael. *Slaying the Dragon: How to Turn Your Small Steps to Great Feats*. New York: HarperCollins Publishers, 1996.

Lewis, Carl, with Jeffrey Marx. *Inside Track: My Professional Life in Amateur Track and Field*. New York: Simon & Schuster, 1990.

Moses, Edwin. "Personal Profile." *Esquire*, June 1988.

Rosenthal, Bert. *Carl Lewis: The Second Jesse Owens*. Chicago: Children's Press, 1984.

Sullivan, George. *Track and Field: Secrets of the Champions*. New York: Doubleday, 1980.

ABOUT THE AUTHOR

Fred McMane has been a journalist for more than 30 years. He was a writer, editor, and administrator for United Press International from 1964–1993, serving as the company's sports editor from 1988–1993. In addition, he has served as a consultant to the Prodigy Services Company and as a copyeditor for the *Newark Star-Ledger*.

Mr. McMane is the author of the following books: *The Baseball Playbook*, with Gil McDougald; *4,192: A Celebration of Pete Rose*; *Amazin': The Story of the 1986 Mets*; *The Worst Day I Ever Had*; *My Hero*; *Winning Women*; and *Scottie Pippen* for Chelsea House's Basketball Legends series.

INDEX